Nature Up Close™

Turtles Up Close

PowerKiDS press™
New York

Katie Franks

Published in 2008 by The Rosen Publishing Group, Inc.
29 East 21st Street, New York, NY 10010

First Edition

Editor: Jennifer Way
Book Design: Kate Laczynski

Photo Credits: All images © Studio Stalio.

Library of Congress Cataloging-in-Publication Data

Franks, Katie.
  Turtles up close / Katie Franks. — 1st ed.
      p. cm. — (Nature up close)
  Includes index.
  ISBN 978-1-4042-4139-8 (library binding)
  1. Turtles—Juvenile literature. I. Title.
  QL666.C5F65 2008
  597.92—dc22
                                          2007019960

Manufactured in the United States of America

Contents

This is a turtle. Turtles are known for moving very slowly.

You can see inside a turtle's body in this picture. A few of a turtle's body parts are its head, heart, **lungs**, and **stomach**.

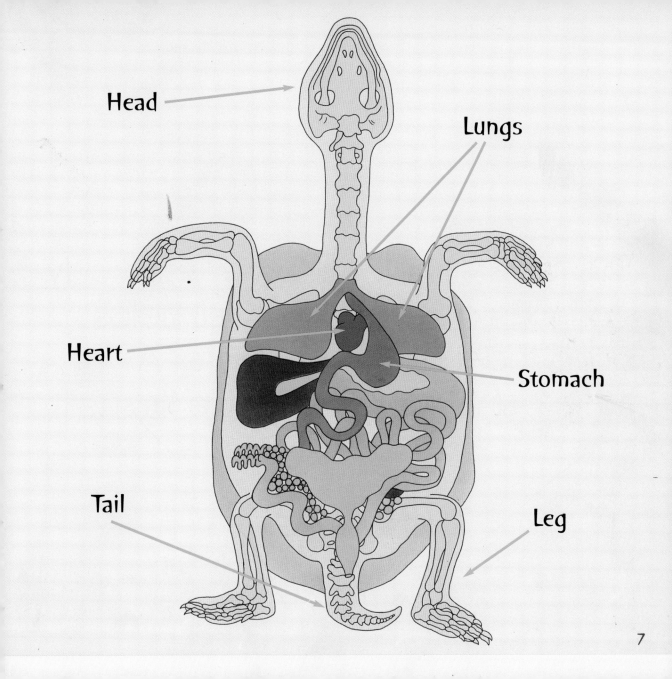

Head

Lungs

Heart

Stomach

Tail

Leg

This turtle's **shell** is shown stomach-side up. The shell helps keep the turtle's body safe. A turtle can even hide inside its shell!

Some kinds of turtles live on land. Other kinds of turtles live underwater.

Sea Turtle

Land Turtle

11

Turtles use their good eyesight and strong nose to hunt for food.

13

Some turtles hunt for fish underwater.

This snapping turtle is hunting a small fish. The turtle uses its wormlike **tongue** to trick the fish into swimming near its mouth.

There are animals that eat turtles.
Sharks sometimes eat sea turtles.

Female, or girl, turtles lay eggs. Baby turtles hatch, or come out, from these eggs.

Laying Eggs

Baby Turtle

People have used turtles' shells to make many things.

Words to Know

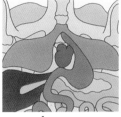

lungs

shell

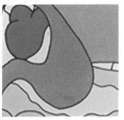

stomach

tongue

Index

Web Sites

Due to the changing nature of Internet links, PowerKids Press has developed an online list of Web sites related to the subject of this book. This site is updated regularly. Please use this link to access the list: www.powerkidslinks.com/nuc/turtle/

24